A ROOKIE BIOGRAPHY

JAMES M. BARRIE

Author of Peter Pan

By Marlene Toby

 Children's Press®

A Division of Grolier Publishing
New York   London   Hong Kong   Sydney
Danbury, Connecticut

James M. Barrie 1860-1937

Library of Congress Cataloging-in-Publication Data

Toby, Marlene.
    James M. Barrie (author of *Peter Pan*) / by Marlene Toby.
      p. cm. — (A Rookie biography)
  Includes index.
  Summary: The life of J. M. Barrie, the creator of *Peter Pan*, told in very simple language
  ISBN 0-516-04271-8
  1. Barrie, J. M. (James Matthew), 1860-1937—Juvenile literature 2. Authors, Scottish—20th Century—Biography—Juvenile literature. 3. Peter Pan (Fictitious character)—Juvenile literature. 4. Children's plays—Authorship—Juvenile literature. [1. Barrie, J. M. (James Matthew), 1860-1937. 2. Authors, Scottish.] I. Title. II. Series: Toby, Marlene. Rookie biography.
PR4076.G73 1995
828 '.91209 — dc20
[B]   95-10107
                                              CIP
                                              AC

482635

James M. Barrie was born in
1860 and died in 1937. He
wrote many plays and books.
His best known play is *Peter
Pan*. This is Mr. Barrie's story.

CONTENTS

The Barrie home in Kirriemuir, Scotland.
James was born in an upstairs room.

Chapter 1

"Just Me"

Day after day, James's mother lay in her bed in the small town of Kirriemuir, Scotland, and cried for her son David. The thirteen-year-old boy had died in an ice-skating accident.

Six-year-old James sat
on the steps leading to
his mother's room and
cried, too. He missed
being with his mother.
Although David had
been the fourth of ten
Barrie children, he was
the mother's favorite.

A few days after David's
funeral, James went into
his mother's room.

Engraving from James Barrie's book, Margaret Ogilvy, *published in 1896*

"Is that you?" she asked. James thought his mother was talking to his dead brother David. "No," he said sadly. "It's just me."

When James's mother heard his words, she called James to her and hugged him. From that time on, her youngest son played an important role in her life.

To make his mother happy,
sometimes James pretended
to be his brother David.
Other times he made up
plays for his mother. Soon
acting and make-believe
came easy for him.

Once James and a friend
made a toy theater and
puppets. They put on plays.
They even charged admission.

A scene in Scotland, where the Barrie family grew up

As James's mother slowly
got over the death of David,
she began spending more
time with James. She
told him stories about
her childhood in Scotland.
They read books together.

Then one day, James had
a wonderful idea. He would
write stories, too! Up to the
attic he ran. From his pen
poured adventure after
adventure.

James put all his favorite
things in his stories —
desert islands, enchanted
gardens, and knights on
black chargers. Then he
read the stories to his mother.

James was happy now.
He thought to himself —
"It's all right to be 'just me.'"

Chapter 2

More Adventures

When James turned thirteen, he went away to school. He thought that he'd have to give up acting out adventure stories. But he was wrong.

At Dumfries Academy, James met Stuart Gordon, also known as Daredevil Dick. Together, they continued the pirate adventures.

At seventeen, James
wrote a play called
Bandelero the Bandit
for the school drama
club. He put all his
favorite characters in
it. He even acted in it.

James was very small
for his age. That is why
he did not play characters
of great size or strength.

PROGRAMME.

To commence this Evening with the *successful* Comedy-Drama entitled

OFF THE LINE !

Harry Coke, an Engine-driver, ...	Mr J. BARRIE.
Jim Brass, his Stoker, ...	Mr L. BENNETT
Lizzie Coke, Harry's wife, ...	... Mr W. ANDERSON
Mary Coke, Harry's sister, ...	Mr H. M'EWEN
Puffy, in love with Mary, ...	Mr G. SMITH

To be followed by *Le Petit Drame Sensational*, in Six Tableaux, entitled

BANDELERO, THE BANDIT.

Bandelero, ...	Mr T. NEWBIGGING
Sir Richard Vernon, ...	Mr H. GRIEVE
Alice, his daughter, ...	... Mr H. M'EWEN
Smike, ... *(his original character)* ...	Mr J. BARRIE
Gamp, ... } Villains { ...	Mr L. BENNETT
Benshaw, ... } Villains { ...	Mr J. BLACKLOCK
Father Dolan, a priest, ...	Mr G. SMITH

To conclude with a Laughable Comedietta, in Two Acts, taken from the
favourite Comedy of

PAUL PRY.

Major-General Johnston, ...	Mr T. NEWBIGGING
Phœbe, his daughter, ...	... Mr J. BARRIE
Old Witherton, ...	Mr J. BLACKLOCK
Mrs Briggs, housekeeper to Witherton, ...	... Mr G. SMITH
Paul Pry, ...	Mr W. ANDERSON
Frank, Witherton's nephew, home from abroad, ...	Mr H. GRIEVE
Simon, Briggs' confidential servant, ...	... Mr J. SMITH
Doubledot, innkeeper, ...	... Mr L. BENNETT

*James acted in all three plays put on by the
Dumfries Amateur Dramatic Club.*

15

James graduated from Edinburgh University (below) at age twenty-two. He got a master's degree.

James left Dumfries
when he was eighteen.
Even though he was
not a good student, his
family wanted him to
continue going to school.
So James went to
Edinburgh University
to study literature.

He did well at
Edinburgh and won
prizes for his writing.
After graduation, he
went back home to be
a writer.

For a while, James
wrote for a small town
newspaper. Then he
began to send articles
to London papers. Some
of the articles were based
on the stories his mother
had told him about the
old days in Scotland.

People liked his stories.
That was all he needed
to know. James packed
up his things and took
the train to London.

*A painting of London, England, in 1902
by Tony Grubhofer*

Chapter 3

Friends

The first few months in
London were not easy.
James was lonely and
could not sell any of his
articles. Still, he made
hard work his friend
and kept on writing.

Three years later,
James's articles were
in important newspapers.

A photograph of James Barrie, taken in 1892

In 1888, James put his
articles about old Scotland
into a book. It sold so well
that he wrote another
book like it. It was called
A Window in Thrums.
It was a best-seller, too.

Barrie made many friends in the theater.
One of them was actress Winifred Emery.

James's third book about
old Scotland was called
The Little Minister. Sales
of this book made him rich.
Now he could visit the
friends he had made and
entertain their children.

James loved children and
had a wonderful way of
drawing them to himself.
His stories were magical.
Through children he
found a way to live out
his childhood adventures.

Mary Ansell (left) and Porthos (right), the dog James bought her

In 1894, James fell in love with Mary Ansell. She was an actress and small, like James. For a wedding present, James bought Mary a big St. Bernard dog. She named the dog Porthos. The family of three settled into their new home in London.

A year later, James's mother died. It was a sad time for him. He said, "Everything I could do for her in this life I have done since I was a boy." In memory of her, James wrote a book. It was called *Margaret Ogilvy*.

The Barries' home at Leinster Corner, near Kensington Park, London

In London James kept up his writing. One day, while walking Porthos in a park called Kensington Gardens, James met three little boys. Their names were George, Jack, and Peter. The two older boys joined James as he played games with Porthos.

Day after day they met. James would tell them stories, and they would act out exciting adventures. James got many story ideas from his visits with them in the garden.

James took many photographs of the Davies boys. Above: George, Jack, and Peter are acting out an adventure. Below: George and Jack are searching for pretend crocodiles.

Even Porthos got into the act. The boys made a tiger mask for him. They pretended to be pirates looking for wild animals.

Then one day James met the boys' mother, Sylvia, at a dinner party. Before long, he was friends with the whole Davies family. From his friendship with them came several books.

In the first book, *The Little White Bird*, James wrote that all the children in London had once been birds in Kensington Gardens.

One of the children, Peter Pan, had flown out of his nursery window and could not get back. Thereafter, he lived in Kensington Gardens with the animals. Thus, the idea for a play called *Peter Pan* was born.

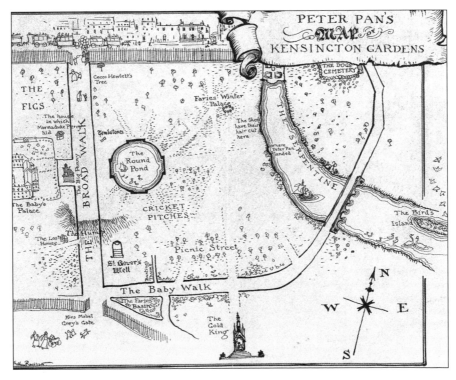

A map of the make-believe world of Peter Pan's Kensington Gardens

Michael Davies as a baby

When the Davies'
fourth son, Michael,
was born, James used
him as a model for the
Peter Pan character.
The other characters in
the play were based on
people James had known.

In the play, the Darling
family was based on the
Davies family. Their
dog Nana was patterned
after Porthos. Wendy
was based on James's
mother, and Captain
Hook was James himself.

An illustration from one of Barrie's books about Peter Pan

*Actress Nina Boucicault played the part of
Peter Pan in 1904.*

Chapter 4

The Dream-Child and a New Family

On November 23, 1903, James began work on a play about Peter Pan. The next day, Sylvia Davies gave birth to her fifth boy, Nico.

Just after Christmas 1904, *Peter Pan* opened in London. James called it his "dream-child." The play was so different that James wondered if people would like it.

It was a great success.
Children loved the fantasy,
and adults in the audience
felt like children again.

*An artist's drawing of Peter Pan and Wendy
flying announced the stage show of* Peter Pan.

*"Where do you live?" Wendy asked.
"Second to the right," said Peter, "and then
straight on till morning."*
    –From The Adventures of Peter Pan, *1911*

Actress Maude Adams played the part of Peter Pan in 1906. In the play, Peter says, "I don't want ever to be a man. I want always to be a little boy and to have fun."

As the years passed, James went on helping adults remember their childhood, and making children happy.

In 1907, Mr. Davies
died. Now the boys
had no father.

James helped the Davies
family all he could. He
bought Mrs. Davies and
the boys a house close
to his and Mary's
house in London.

Then two years later,
Mary and James were
divorced, and Mrs.
Davies became very
ill. In May 1910,
Mrs. Davies died.

After that, James
became the sole
support of the boys.

One by one, James's
boys were growing up.
George, Jack, and Peter
went away to school.
A loyal nursemaid took
care of the two youngest
boys in the family home.

James often visited ten-
year-old Michael and
seven-year-old Nico.
He wrote letters to
the older boys.

Chapter 5

Forever Young

In 1914, World War I
changed everyone's lives.
George and Peter joined
the army. Jack was
already in the navy.

In March 1915, James
wrote George that he
surely hoped "that we
may all be together
again once at least."

Opposite page: Cartoons of James Barrie appeared often in London's Punch *magazine.*

FORTH from that beetling brain, so
much like Zeus's,
  Sprang Fancy armed with pen of gold
To battle with the worst of life's abuses—
  Our silly way of growing old.
If there exists another Bart
With Barrie's trick of magic art,
Or if there breathes a second O.M.
Who could have made his *Peter* poem,
Give me their names; I'd like to know 'em.

MR. PUNCH'S PERSONALITIES.

VII.—SIR JAMES BARRIE, BART., O.M.

That was never to be.
Four days after James
sent his letter, he learned
that George had been
killed. Soon after, Peter
came home to recover
from the stress of war.

The war ended in 1918.
James kept writing.
Jack got married, and
Michael went off to school
at Oxford University.

In May 1921, Michael
drowned while swimming.
Michael had been
James's favorite boy.
After his death, James
was never the same.

"Michael was pretty
much my world...,"
he said. "What
happened [to him]
was in a way the
end of me."

After the Davies
boys married and
moved away, James
lived alone in his
London apartment.

For the next sixteen
years he continued to
write and make friends
of important people. He
helped many children.

*Opposite page: James Barrie with two young
actresses outside Dumfries Academy in 1924*

When James Barrie died
on June 21, 1937, Nico
and Peter were with him.

James Barrie had wanted
to stay young forever, and
he left the world a boy who
did — Peter Pan.

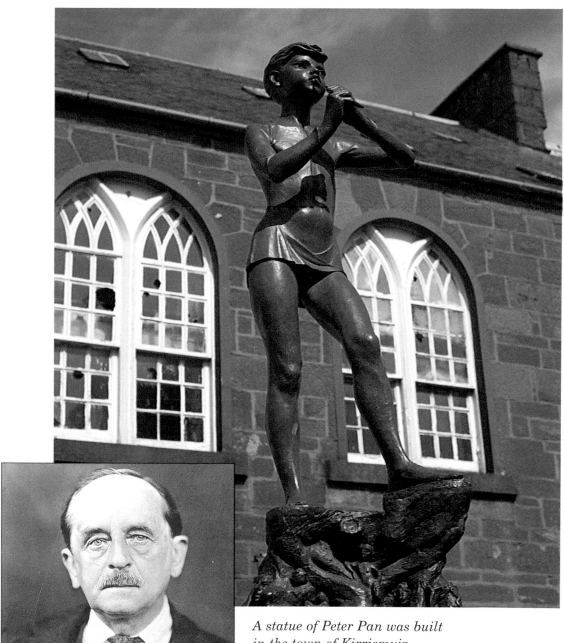

A statue of Peter Pan was built
in the town of Kirriemuir,
Scotland, in honor of James
Barrie and in memory of the
magical character he created
for children of the world.

Important Dates

1860   May 9 — Born at Kirriemuir, Scotland,
        to Margaret Ogilvy and David Barrie

1873   Went to Dumfries Academy

1878   Went to Edinburgh University

1884   Moved to London, England

1891   *The Little Minister* was published

1894   Married Mary Ansell

1897   Met the Llewelyn Davies boys

1904   *Peter Pan* opened in England

1909   Divorced from Mary

1910   Became responsible for the Llewelyn
        Davies boys

1915   George Llewelyn Davies killed in France

1921   Michael Llewelyn Davies drowned
        at Oxford

1937   June 19 — Died in London, England

Index

Page numbers in boldface type indicate illustrations.

So Percy's family sat on the beach
where the water was warm,
the sand was soft,
where breezes blew,
and waves crashed over the rocks,
and had a picnic after all.

"What's this?" asked Grandpa.
"Peanuts!" said Percy's sister.
"Popcorn!" cried Percy's brother.
"And peaches!" said Mother.

Percy's family came back from their swim.

There were pickles and peanuts and cherries and peas;
biscuits, bananas, and crackers and cheese.

Soon there was lots of food.

He took a large doughnut out of his bag
and set it on the plate in front of Grizzly.

A police officer was strolling along the boardwalk.
"Say!" he said. "I'll bet those bears would like a doughnut."

And he gave the whole box to Blackie.

"Hey!" cried a swimmer, who was dripping wet.
"They can have my popcorn!"

"Maybe they'd like one of my hot dogs," he said
and put it on Panda's plate.

A lifeguard wearing sunglasses stopped and looked at the bears.

She took three peaches from a bag
and placed them in front of Teddy.

Pretty soon a grandma in a big straw hat stopped
and smiled at Percy's bears.
"I do believe those bears would like some peaches," she said.

He took the red-checked napkins and
tied them around the bears' necks.
He put an empty plate in front of each.
Then, on the boardwalk, he printed in large letters,
Please DO feed the bears.

Percy's hungry, grumpy family went for one last swim,
trying not to think of lunch.
Go home early? Percy thought. *No way!*
He looked at his bears.
He looked at the cooler.

"Oh, Percy!" said Mother.
"What will we eat?" cried his sister.
"I'm hungry!" wailed his brother.
"Well, we've had a nice morning. I guess
  we'll just have to head home early,"
  said Grandpa.

"Time to eat!" called Mother,
   as she spread out the blanket.
"Come and get it!" yelled Grandpa.
   Everyone sat down.
   Father opened the picnic cooler.

At the beach,
Percy waded in the warm water.
He dug in the soft sand.
He flew his kite in the breeze
and climbed on the rocks.

They headed for the beach where the water was warm,
the sand was soft,
where breezes blew,
and waves crashed over the rocks.

Everyone squeezed
and squirmed
and turned
and twisted
until the whole family was in the car.

Soon it was time to go.

So Percy left something behind.

Percy saw his old black bear there on the steps.
"Can I bring Blackie with us?" he asked.
"Not one more thing!" said Grandpa.
"Once we pack the cooler, that's all the room there is.
If you brought your black bear, we'd have to
leave something behind."

So Percy left something behind.

Percy went out to the car.
Grandpa was packing the trunk.
He was pushing things around,
trying to make room for a big umbrella.
They were going to the beach where
the water was warm, the sand was soft,
and where breezes blew.

So Percy left something behind.

Percy went into the bedroom.
His sister was packing her radio.
They were going to the beach where the water
was warm and the sand was soft.
Percy saw his grizzly bear on the rug.

"Can I take Grizzly with us?" he asked.
"There isn't room!" said his sister.
"If we took your grizzly, we'd have to
  leave something behind."

Percy saw his panda bear under the sink.
"Can I take Panda with us?" he asked.
"There isn't room!" said his brother.
"Look at all the stuff we have to take!
If we took your panda, we'd have to
leave something behind."

So Percy left something behind.

Percy went into the bathroom.
His brother was packing his flippers.
They were going to the beach
where the water was warm.

"Can I take Teddy with us?" he asked.
"Your teddy, to the beach?" said Father.
"Why, we barely have room for the cooler.
 If we took your teddy, we'd have to leave
 something behind."

Percy's family was going to the beach.
They were going to have a picnic,
and Father was bringing his folding chair.
Percy saw his teddy bear by the sofa.

phyllis reynolds naylor

please DO
feed the bears

illustrated by
ana lópez escrivá

atheneum books for young readers

NEW YORK   LONDON   TORONTO   SYDNEY   SINGAPORE

To my second granddaughter, Tressa Clarice Naylor,

my birthday buddy

—P. R. N.

To Sandra and her family, and to my parents

—A. L. E.

Atheneum Books for Young Readers
An imprint of Simon & Schuster Children's Publishing Division
1230 Avenue of the Americas
New York, New York 10020
Text copyright © 2002 by Phyllis Reynolds Naylor
Illustrations copyright © 2002 by Ana López Escrivá

The text of this book is set in Futura MD BT.
The illustrations are rendered in acrylic paint.
Printed in Hong Kong
First Edition
2 4 6 8 10 9 7 5 3 1
Library of Congress Cataloging-in-Publication Data
Naylor, Phyllis Reynolds.
Please do feed the bears / written by Phyllis Reynolds Naylor ;
illustrated by Ana López Escrivá.—1st ed.
p.   cm.
Summary: Percy almost ruins the family picnic at the beach when he insists on bringing
all his large teddy bears along, but his ingenuity saves the day.
ISBN 0-689-82561-7
[1. Picnicking—Fiction. 2. Teddy bears—Fiction. 3. Toys—Fiction.
4. Animals—Fiction. 5. Beaches—Fiction.] I. Escrivá, Ana López, ill. II. Title.
PZ7.N24 Pi 2002
[E]—dc21   00-056573

And after dinner

she toasted Daddy.

there's a gorilla war.

Daddy says
he has trees
for all his shoes.

Daddy says
lions pray on

other animals.

Daddy says there should

be more car pools.

Mommy says her

favorite painter is Dolly.

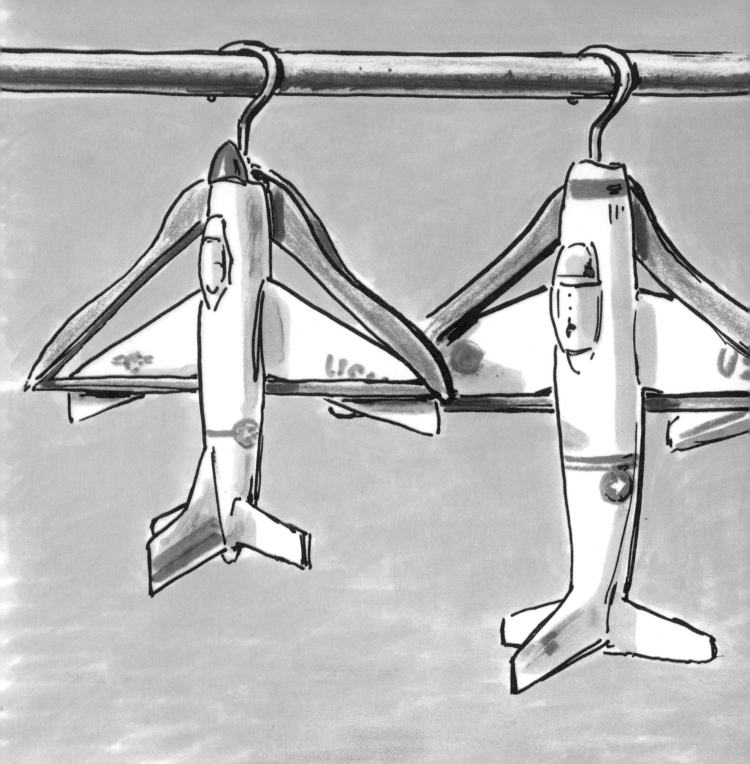

**Mommy says
there are airplane hangers.**

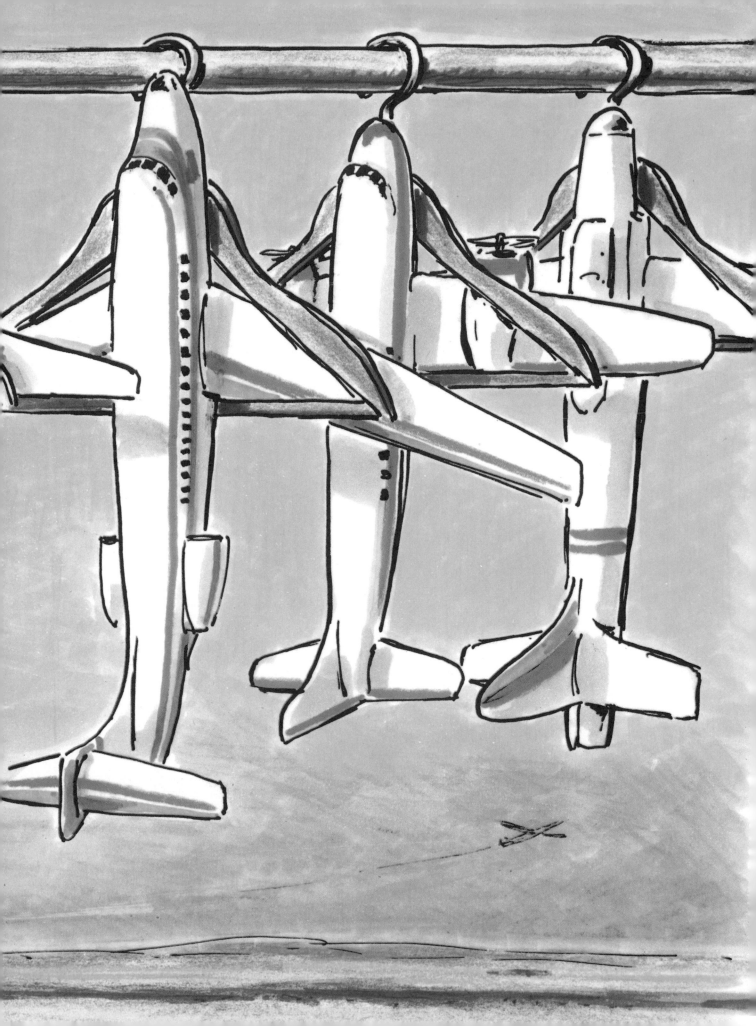

Daddy says he has the best fishing tackle.

It says on TV
a man held up a bank.

He spent two years in the pen.

**And he has just escaped
and is now on the lamb.**

At the ocean Daddy says

watch out for the under toe.

Daddy says he plays the piano by ear.

Daddy says that in college

people row in shells.

**And some row
in a single skull.**

Mommy says she's going to tell me about Santa Claws.

And Daddy says he's going to tell me the story of

the tortoise and the hair.

Stories like these drive me up a wall!